BERN

All you need to create a world is some crayons. Hare and Bear have a whole box of colored crayons and lots of ideas. In this book they show you how to draw a boat. If you watch how Hare and Bear do it, you can draw one too. Just copy the shapes from the colored box at the top of each page onto your own drawings. And soon you'll be sailing the waves.

Hare and Bear Draw A Boat

Diann Timms

Reader's Digest Kids
Pleasantville, N.Y.–Montreal

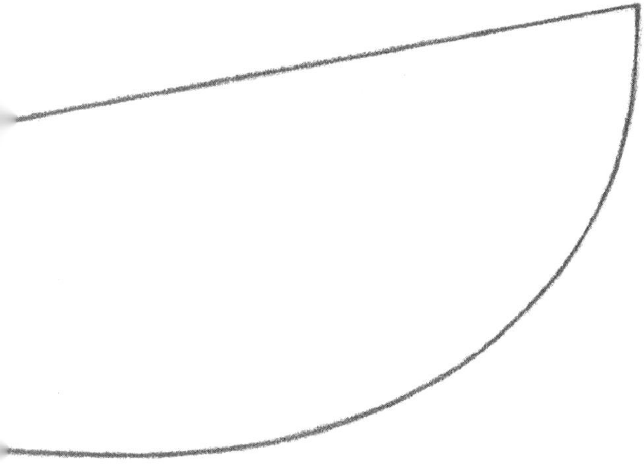

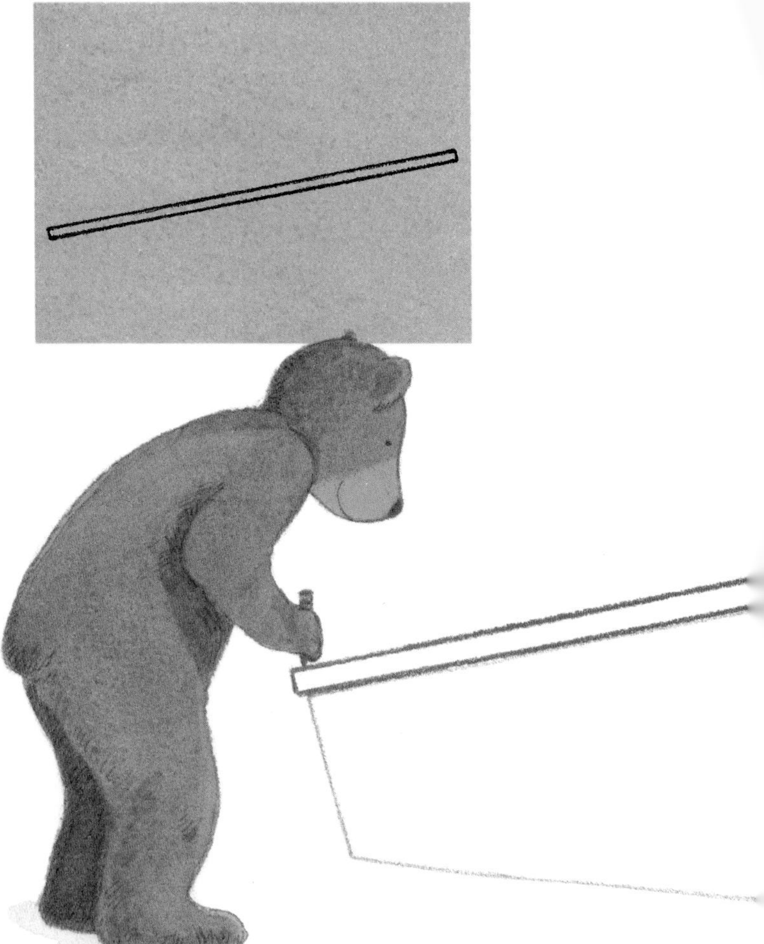

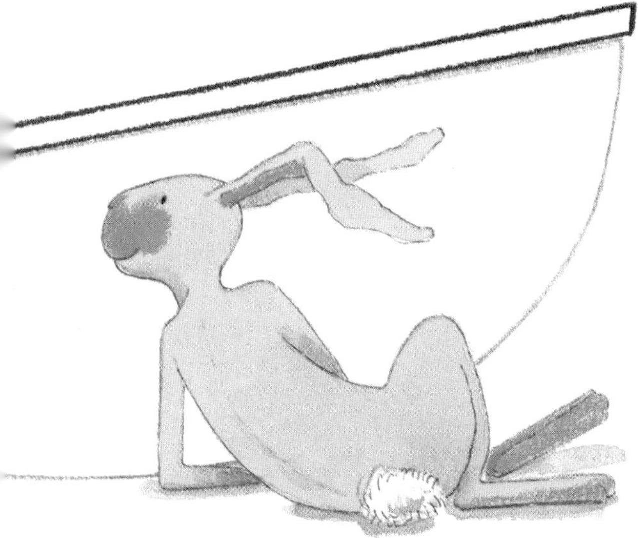

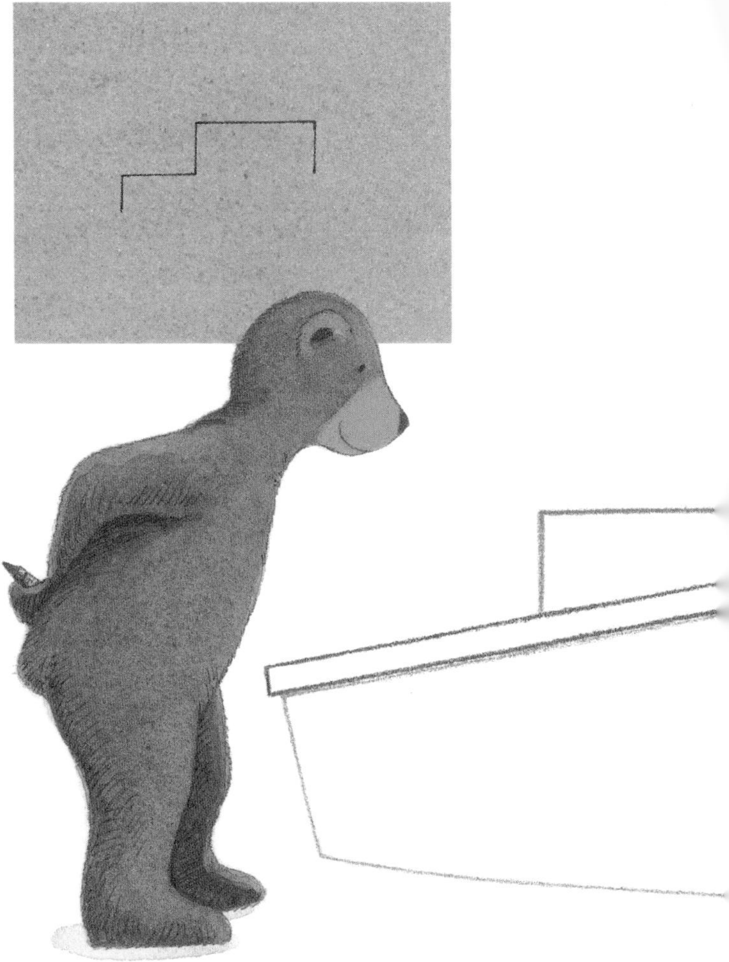

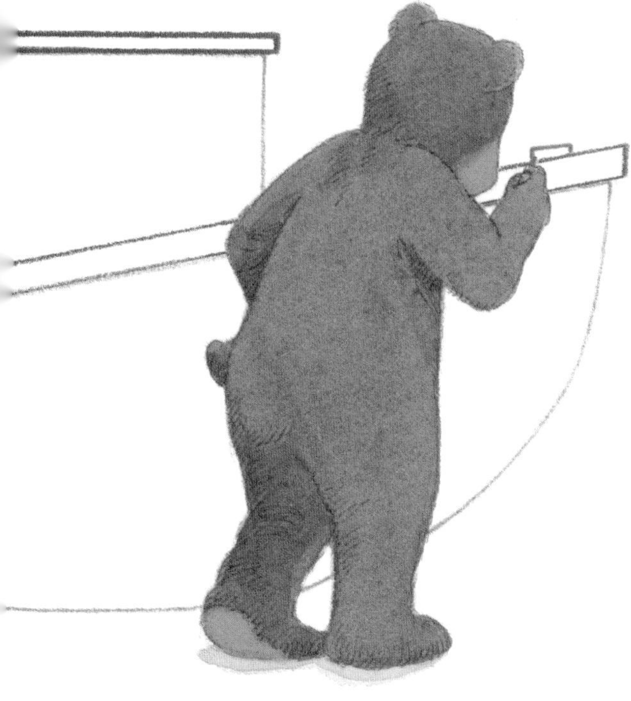

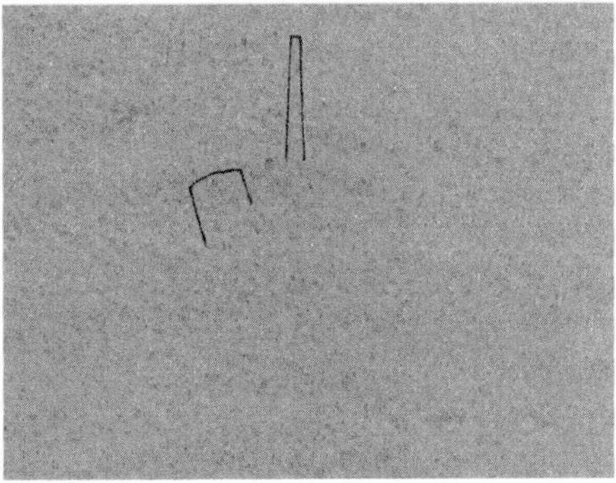

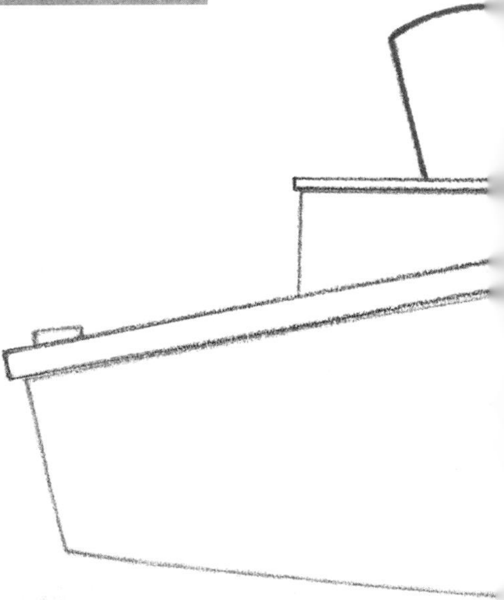

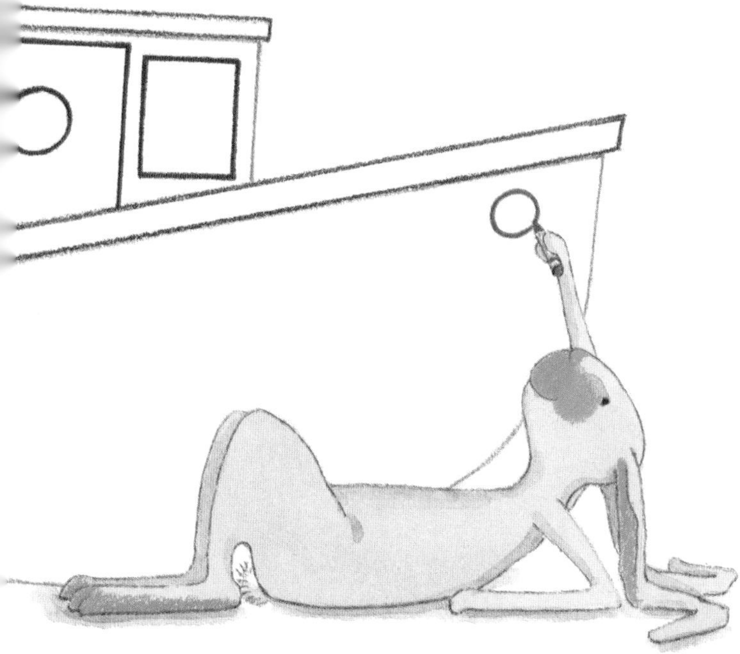

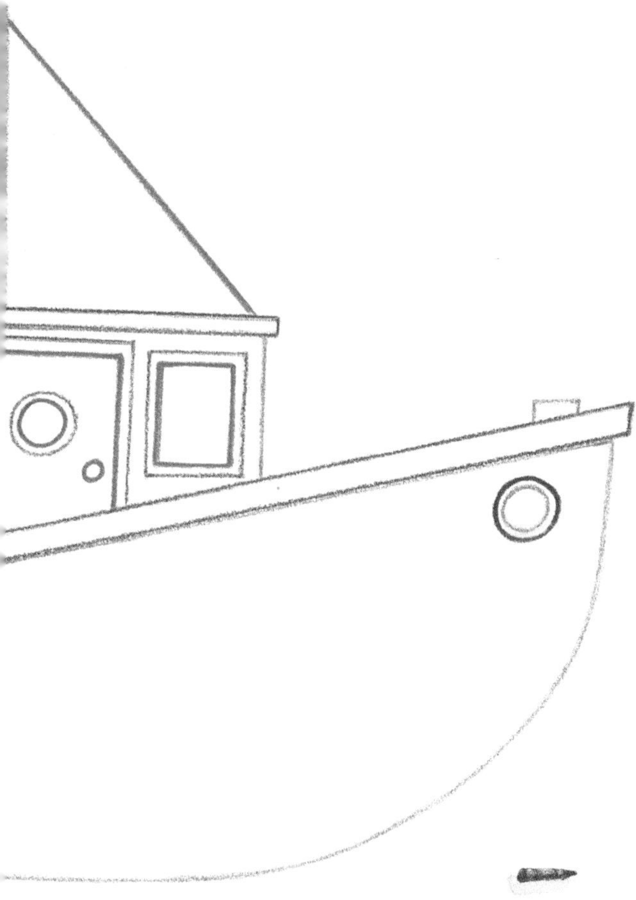

What shall we draw next?

A Reader's Digest Kids Book
Conceived by Diann Timms and Delian Bower Publishing

Library of Congress Cataloging in Publication data applied for.

ISBN 0–89577–534–4 (v. 5)

ISBN 0–89577–548–4 (set)

Reader's Digest

Printed in the United States of America

99 98 97 96 95 94 10 9 8 7 6 5 4 3 2 1

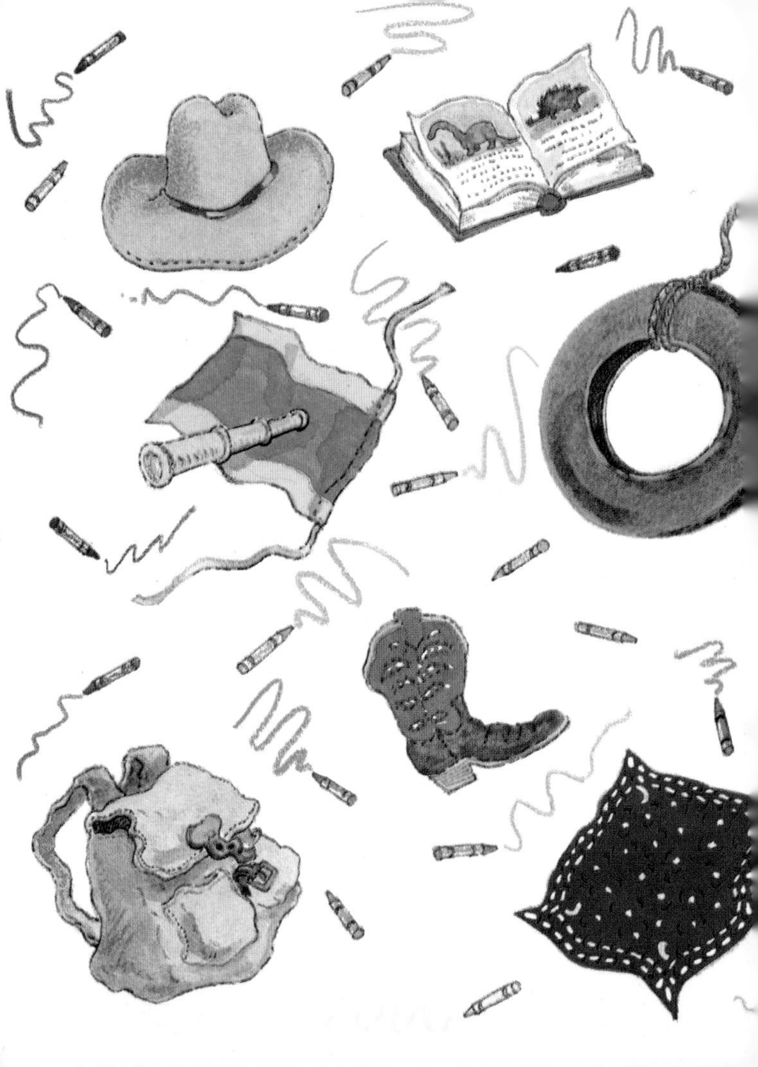